Blue Sunrise

by

Bert Almon

Book design and cover by Neil Wagner.

Published Spring 1980 by

Thistledown Press

668 East Place

Saskatoon, Saskatchewan

Canada   S7J 2Z6

Canadian Cataloguing in Publication Data

Almon, Bert, 1943-
    Blue sunrise

    Poems.
    ISBN 0-920066-30-5 bd.
    ISBN 0-920066-29-1 pa.

    I. Title.
PS8551.L59B58   C811'.54   C80-091016-8
PR9199.3.A45B58

ACKNOWLEDGMENTS

Most of the poems in this book have appeared in the following literary magazines and journals:

ANTIGONISH REVIEW

ARIEL

THE BARD

THE BLACKBIRD CIRCLE

CANADIAN FORUM

CONCERNING POETRY

COPPERFIELD

DESCANT

EVENT

THE FIDDLEHEAD

GRAIN

LAKEHEAD UNIVERSITY REVIEW

LOCO MOTIVES

NEW ORLEANS REVIEW

PERMAFROST

PRIME CUTS

QUARRY

RAPPORT

ROCKY MOUNTAIN REVIEW

THE SALT CEDAR

"Hurrying Nature" first appeared in THREE MOUNTAINS PRESS ANTHOLOGY (1976).
"For Nancy Going to War" is included in ANTHOLOGY EIGHTY (Hurtig).

Some of the poems were also broadcast on CBC Anthology.

This book has been published with the assistance of Alberta Culture and The Canada Council.

TABLE OF CONTENTS

I

II.

for Barbara

For Nancy Going to War

ten above on Boxing Day
a break in the cold
I drove south to Calgary
                    a girl and her police dog
                    snow currents swirling over their feet
                    good company for a sleepy driver

the girl was Nancy
                just over eighteen and wearing
"one pair of tights
long underwear
two pairs of pants
two sweaters
one scarf
one parka
and it turned out warm"

the dog was Maggie
                ten months old and wearing
her own fur
          sleeping peacefully on the floor
          soft snout benign against my foot

we fogged up the windows with talk
Nancy wiped them with her scarf
                    everything was far-out
she wrote down the books I mentioned
on the flyleaf of *The Prophet*
                notebook addressbook and Bible
"You've read it?
          it's so beautiful
              you've read *The Little Prince?*
              far-out

do you eat brown rice?
did you know meat is poison?

                what I like is doing acid
                running out of the house
                hugging the first person I see
                far-out"

she took off the parka and one sweater
                      relief in the stuffy car
"do you like going naked?
                it's so natural
you forget some people don't like it
you can even get arrested
it's like a real war sometimes
but we'll win   we've got love
they can't fight that"
                then it was the crossroads
                she put on the sweater and parka
                said thank you and got out

I left her standing on the shoulder
thumbing her way to the free life on the coast
or an asteroid with a magic flower

the hip middle class calls it the Children's Crusade
says far-out with a straight face
not remembering any history
                but I've met enough pirates
                and slave merchants on the roads
to wish Nancy had more armor
and Maggie was a little fiercer

Edmonton/Calgary, December 26, 1970

9

This Day in History

The radio tells me
that back in 1950
the sun rose blue
over Great Britain,
from forest fires
in Western Canada.
I know the dust of
exploding Krakatoa
gave the whole world
a year of fine sunsets.

I try to imagine
whose labor I lift
on my fork, what
ashes sift in my tea,
and get about as far
as the corner market.
We can say "brother"
to everyone, but
only a blue sunrise
might make us feel it.

Bodhisattva's Head. Cameron Library

A head broken off, battered limestone
with heavy-lidded eyes and a forehead jewel
of enlightenment surmounting the Greek features
which argue that the chisel outlasted
Alexander's sword. This figure of compassion
a British major with a hyphenated name
bought in the Khyber Pass — a rifle paid
to a tribesman. The Bodhisattva's career
of kindness descends to the card catalogue
where it rests, a spent projectile, one touch
of benign influence at the mouth verging
on a smile, as if the head contemplated
its own history: the invasion of motifs
and the trade routes of violence, vandalism
rewarded by connoisseurship, sanctity
and imperialism. Ways of the world.
Liberation is another: breath on these lips.

Remedial English

Hong Kong is a crowded ship that will beach
on the shores of China when the British lease expires.
Early refugees double-moonlight to raise their fees
for the universities of North America, where
they thumb dictionaries to get through Shakespearean
tragedy and Depression novels set in Saskatchewan.
Marking the less grammatical papers, you think
the red pencil is an oar blade coming down hard
on hands that cling to the side of a small boat.

A Studio

I should admire your artful artlessness:
uneven forms, the finish marked with cracks
and bubbles, and I should admire your speed,
the way you slap the clay like a doctor
delivering triplets, child after child.
A full shelf means a full artist. Yet I've heard
about a craftsman who takes his work to sea,
applying lacquer where no dust can stick
to the bright surface. You might call his pains
excessive, but he'd call them just enough.

Growth Factors

suburbs

The builders shear off the sod,
the landscapers buy it cheap
and haul it away in trucks.
The new owner looks over
his yard, a swamp or desert,
and pays a high price for soil
trucked in by the landscapers.

country

"The people who owned these woods
kept horses, so every year
they would burn the underbrush
to make the grass grow thicker.
Some trees still show the tide marks
of fire on their trunks. That must
be why we have no fruitful
or interesting bushes now."

city

It was a big empty yard
twenty five years ago, with
a few seedlings sparsely placed.
You'd doubt their shadows would
ever touch. Now a Nanking
cherry tree tangles branches
with a broad elder, maple
grips maple, one evergreen
has climbed thirty feet for air.
It's entirely human, failing
to foresee life choking life.

Sleeping on the Slope

Brightness keeps prying at my eyes
   and every breeze in the spruce
      sounds like a squad car on gravel

Cops woke us up last night
   asked my age, my friend's age
      missed the bottle melting in the fire

Do I belong here, restless eyes
   putting the scene on postcards
      something for the pocket, captioned:

The popular blue lakes, under
   a peak topped with permanent snows
      all like technicolor to me

If I were a fossil here
   long print on precambrian rock
     I could lie in sleep

a light tracing, kiss-on-stone
   lost in the dancing lattice
      of branches in the wind

A Month in a Small Town

Call it Paradise, Alskatchewan
                              a name lifted
from the Chamber of Commerce folders
it was surrounded by fields of wheat and oil
(the pumps stand in meadows nodding their heads
like faithful donkeys)
                          it had broad streets
with no traffic and a church on every corner
there was a single school where she came to teach
In the classroom closet
                          a hat, coat, briefcase
left by the previous teacher
                              who'd loaded his car
in a hurry one night and disappeared
He turned up in Las Vegas
dealing blackjack for the mob
to calm his nerves

There was a paper that printed only the good news
and a movie house to show the choicest Westerns
the opera company put on the latest Gilbert & Sullivan
among all those churches two religions flourished
those who went to Sunday school on Sunday
those who went to the bar on Friday nights
both sects could boast perfect attendance
more than the school could do

In despair she joined the wet denomination
but one night the town butcher, foamy-faced
emerged from the bar smoke to make a pass
fondling her haunches like a pair of prize hams
she gave up
                drove out of town on the narrow highway
and saw no flaming sword at the city limits
just the statue for the valiant early settlers
who could stick it out
                          in the rear view mirror
a glimpse of a flare in the gas field
the iron spire tipped with a hellish torch

16

The Woman in Plaid

She calls me a chameleon,
colorful and lively with others,
slow and somber with her.

It's just the familiar joke:
against her crazy quilt
of kaleidoscopic feeling

I turn gray in defeat,
wrapped in exhausted skin,
looking for a way to bolt

to an even monochrome.

Etchings

old salt

The sexy tattoo
on the old sailor's forearm:
a woman in a daring bathing dress
from 1925.

rule of thumb

When I went out with callipygian Caroline,
my friend Chuck gave me a warning: take a look
at her mother, he said, in ten years she'll be
just as wide, it's a sure thing. Twelve years later
I met Chuck again, and noted that his own wife
is slender, but Chuck is as bald as his father.

the mainliner

When she comes in, tired and quiet, glassy-eyed,
her mother gets out the pamphlet on drug abuse
to check for symptoms of uppers and downers,
on the lookout for those telltale needlemarks.
Thank God for the *Parental Guide to Dangerous Drugs:*
twenty years ago what mother would have missed
the signs of love, that perilous intoxication.

Southpaw's Paranoia

Growing up lefthanded.
you always feel wrong
the bad penmanship
a signed confession

Going to Miss Slaughter
for extra practice
she sighed and said
"You never learned to print
why should you practice script?
I tried to teach your mother
she was lefthanded too"

Or the doctor dipping
gauze into plaster
"Aren't you lucky
it's just the left arm
a nasty break like this"

And the years of botchery
with scissors and canopeners
meant for Righty
and the guitar manuals
you have to read backward
there are skills in life
you'll never master
rules in life
you never understand
until you get it all wrong
"Hey, you can't do it that way"
from the eternal shop teacher

There's your mother's saying
"If you're not careful
one of these mornings
you'll wake up dead"
a lefthanded maxim
if you've ever heard one —

The Unveiling

Shaving my beard I thought I'd find out
how much the years have added to my face —
time and experience like touchy artists
worked silently behind a bristly curtain.
The blunt scissors tugged, the shaver head
grew hot from overuse, till the beard lay
in the basin, and the face in the mirror
was young, skin like a baby's to the touch.
Disgusted, I turned on both faucets, watching
the lukewarm water swirl the whiskers down
the drain, some clinging to the porcelain —
perhaps the few strands of wisdom and age.

Holocaust

A picnic game: the egg toss
a dozen couples, two rows
throwing white vials of protein
back and forth, moving apart
one short step each time, until
the eggs begin to shatter:
a rich smear of yellow lies
on the sidewalk, sticky threads
of albumen drip from hands
when an egg disintegrates
from the impact of a catch

In a few minutes, one pair
grins in triumph, hands unsoiled
among the sheepish, giggling
losers, if there are losers
here in a land of plenty
where one victorious egg
is returned to the carton

Going Under

1

Your lights some miles north
of everyone, in cold and
unfamiliar waters.
We left you alone, thinking
you'd make it, even the flares
we took for fireworks. Then
no lights, and silence on the radio.

2

The police found her wandering
in the street, unable to speak,
her purse filled with money
and letters to friends, unmailed.
Like a patrol coming across
an empty lifeboat, fully-provisioned.

The Wrong Side of the Bed

Linoleum creaking underfoot
clear sticky dishes, eat old bread
one more cup soaked from the teabag

Pale roses dangle from the vase
stems sucking water, buds broken
to a brief bloom in electric light

Tea leaves leak from the bag
beware of scissors they whisper
look out for falling petals

Pop Mysticism

I remember the first time
hearing Cohen's *Suzanne*
with a roomful of reverent people
who sat hushed as the needle lifted
till someone spoke up
"That reminds me
of what my father
used to say:
Nothing can turn my stomach
except a woman's belly
against my back"

The Squint

By a fault in the lens curvature
images float before the retina,
and even when the world is framed
in a rectangle of sharpened sight,
the brain has the habits of the defect:
it wants the salient detail, as if
it had to squint to bring anything
into focus from a myopic blur.

So I look for significant items,
images that serve as handtrucks
for concepts: sea foam dissipating
on the shore means whatever I feel
as impermanent at that instant.
But it's the panoramic vision
I admire, for which the pattern
and not the detail is salient.
It takes in the whole landscape,
the way the ocean shifts colours
with the composition of shoreline
and the contours of its bed. Pure
delight in the accidents of form,
all meaning sunk into the pattern.
I admire those far-sighted poets
who might have been painters.

What Takes Us Now

1

The brook was a seam of ice
through the trees, and near it
we found a coyote, frozen
in a leghold trap. The farmer
neighboring this land forgets
who owns it now. He digs up
small birches for his front yard,
and protects his lambs. My friend
doesn't believe in boundaries,
so she'll argue with him
over the danger to her dog,
and the balance of nature,
sketching mice in red ink.
Birds pecked at slabs of fat
she hung from the birches.
Frost twinkled on the coyote's fur.

2

On the way to town that night, just past
the egg factory, I saw a snow plow
plowing the dry pavement. Sparks flew up,
a sterile sowing, undeniably beautiful.

Breakfast at Angelo's

The sign over the door has a winged urchin
in a long nightshirt blowing a trumpet.
Angelo serves me coffee in a styrofoam cup
and a misshapen doughnut on tissue paper.
A one-armed man in sneakers and a tweed suit
is mopping the floor. Mostly he just stirs
the bucket, and a patron makes a little joke,
"You're going to wear out the handle first."
Everybody laughs: the sleepy night watchman,
the whores just off the graveyard shift, everyone
but the simple man near the back, who sings
Silent Night in the middle of April. I wish
I could write glibly about the lives of the poor,
the class struggle, but no one here admits
to poverty, and the owner is as poor as the rest.

Afterward I walk past the finance companies,
the pawnshops filled with rings, watches, guns,
all neatly arranged behind barred windows.
An Indian overtakes me, his pigtails tucked
into a tattered silk shirt patterned with
standing polar bears. In the display case
of the raw fur store, a beaver crouches
on a log, wary, his glass eyes gleaming,
unaware that someone skinned him long ago.

Morning/Cedar Waxwings

Warm tongues of air rise from the bedroom floor
to lick me pillowed here by the window.
Beyond in the subzero, waxwings mill
in maple branches, their gray feathers fluffed
against the cold. One hops toward the glass
on a narrow path, then stops, eyes intent
under the topknot, so near that I can see
the red droplets on his wings as I move
close to the window, permitting myself
no excitement, knowing that one deep breath
would fog the hard clarity between us.

Weather Lore

Three infallible signs
that winter's here:

this morning, milk bottles
frozen in the chute

this afternoon, the door jammed
by creeping frost

tonight in bed, a woman wearing
only my woolen socks

31

December Pastimes

The reach of my domestic lore
is *bring the pot to the kettle,*
not the kettle to the pot,

and as I drink my tea
on a snowy night, I hear
the sound of thread

being drawn through cloth
across the table from me.
The pages of my book make

a noise, the spoon in the cup
rattles, but her sound shapes
a picture, a basket of flowers

in five colors. Outside,
the wind is scattering flakes.
Inside, spring is growing

on a white field.

Up Against It

This chilled humiliation,
stuck in a few inches of snow
outside my own garage,
exhaust fumes turning the white
as dirty as a smoker's lungs.

I know the pattern:
cold air from the arctic vortex
presses down on us,
all relief comes from the coast,
Pacific disturbances —

but the vortex that counts
right now is a spinning tire
tossing away cardboard,
ground clay from the cat's box,
and nothing works but to go deeper,

rock into a rut
long enough for the tires to catch.
Here we live, between the pole
and the winds, back and forth
the mercury moves, conditions of life

on a slightly tilted turning planet.

A Trace of Resin

My wife and I lay 2 x 4's
in the garage, a border for
the new blacktop. Sawdust
and a trace of resin
in the air. We work well
together: I drive nails
a little straighter, she
saws boards precisely.
The bubble floats centered
in the spirit level.
My lefthandedness,
her rightness, serve us well
hammering at the corners.
We balance each other
in this minor instance too.
Long ago we learned what
the two sexes are for.

Cease Fire/Schwegers' Farm

The inversion layer claps a dome
of yellow smoke over the city
we breathe our own wastes
blood craves adulterous ties
with carbon monoxide, spurns
lawful bonds with oxygen

So we drive away from the fumes
to colder, cleaner air, out
to the forty acres of our friends
for a day of country leisure

But children will skate
even if the frozen pond
bears nine inches of snow
I take a small bent shovel
half an hour of clearing
and I've prepared a surface
ample for figure-skating mice

Then the roar of a motor
violates the rural peace
Charlie with a snow blower
round the rink he goes
a twenty-foot geyser of white
spouts from the iron chariot
of a storm god with ice crystals
in his beard, then thunder chokes,
sputters out, the tank run dry
but the pond is clear enough
we drag the dead engine home

Inside by the fireplace
I fill my own tank with food
and watch the light glistening
on polished boards of the walls
my cramped muscles suggesting
a truce with internal combustion

Hurrying Nature

Small earthen barges
ferry the flowers
over the cold spring
of a northern climate.

We outwit the short
growing season, sunning
the plants on the porch,
bringing them in at night.

When patience gives out,
we shift green cargoes
to flower beds, a risky way
to hasten their growth.

Still, I notice a bee
probing the sealed buds
of one little salvia
before my wife can even

finish covering the roots.

Moving Down

This is the absolute withdrawal
you find yourself on the glacier
the ice a thousand feet thick
blue crystals six inches across
winter in the height of summer
you shrink into a naked worm
pollen-eater, the wind feeds you
with the bounty of richer regions

This is your last form, new eyes
a single layer of cells aching
with the bright blue light, seeing
a way to the final descent
a crevasse to the lower layer
where ice turns pliable under pressure
from such depths the moving stars
grow visible in the heart of day

and you see they all have faces

37

Storm. Lake Kananaskis

Sitting with friends in this tent
the lamp roars while the rain sizzles
running off the swaying walls

Closing my eyes I can feel
the flapping tent ascend
a canvas bird clearing the mountains!

Pool Notes

A lifeguard is a petty god
with silver whistle and a tall chair
The bikinied girls find reasons
to stand and talk with him
A drowner would be out of luck
hidden by a wall of nubility

Heads bob in sun-spattered waves
a bodiless transfiguration
A black child floats at poolside
She studies the water inlet closely
showing an orange tongue
where clear water enters blue

Leech Gathering

The most turbid water I've seen since
the Great Salt Lake, dead heart of Utah.
But this soup has living ingredients:
weeds, minnows, bugs and tiny frogs,
all stirring in a thick green broth.
I'm on the lake shore with a salt cellar,
watching the children swim in a fence
of rope buoyed by empty plastic bottles,
bleach and soap. When the children get out,
tired of swimming in muck, I inspect
their feet for stowaways, black leeches
fastened with a soft, persistent kiss.
A boy has one, four inches at least,
clinging to the back of his right leg
and he twitches in panic as I try
to shake salt on the creature. Mutter
of old proverbs about moving targets.
Finally I hit it, the thing falls off
and contracts to a round, black circle,
the small purse of a miserly vampire.
The boy trips over the cellar, knocking it
into the water. I bring it up, but
the crystals have fled. With ceremony
I unscrew the lid and pour the water back.
I christen this the lesser salt lake.
You won't find it on the official maps.

The Trackers

The man from Ohio wonders at the wildlife
here in Alberta: in Cleveland he sees
nothing but pigeons, sparrows and guard dogs.
We take an amble down the acreage trail,
spotting birds, puzzling out the tracks.
He wants some excitement and inspects
a large print, thinking it must be bear.
I know it isn't — it could be a dog, a big one.
He won't believe me, but he hasn't seen a bear
outside a city zoo. I point to a black, oval
dropping as a diversion, claiming it's the huge egg
of a Canadian mosquito. He's been to Texas once:
no fooling him when he's following bear tracks.
Around a corner we come upon the bruin, a snarling
Labrador retriever. A bear would probably run away,
the dog advances.
                 We take up the healthy sport
of jogging, and I can hardly find the breath
to shout that we might have had this experience
on the paved streets of Dayton or Cleveland.

The Accident

1

I lay another useless blanket on the child
and pick up her coins from the dark pavement,
while the driver keeps asking, "Is she breathing,
is she breathing?" Who can I give the money to?
A man with presence of mind brings a flashlight,
and begins to direct the traffic around us.

2

Drinking my midnight, I watch the kitten
crouched under a sheet of newspaper,
poising to pounce on my bare feet, leaping,
claws drawn in, running when I grab his tail
under the low refuge of an easy chair.
My wife and daughters are asleep.
I turn off lights as I walk toward them,
moving with the darkness at my back,
thinking of a house where no one is sleeping.

The Rules of Venery

Calling her evasive, you raid her secrets,
so she runs about like an anxious plover
leading you from one false nest to another,

chirping *here, over here,* far from the spot
where the helpless feelings are huddled.
The relentless hunter bags no birds, I say,

and when you turn to making nets, take a hint:
leave a flaw in the weaving, the spell requires
an open gate to let the Mother Spider out.

November 4

I had scribbled it large
on the desk calendar:
RAKE THE LEAVES TODAY
but the morning light
through the curtains
seemed too strong
When you looked out
and said "oh no"
I knew right away —
another early winter

For once the snow
hasn't bothered me
It didn't stick
to the sidewalks
and my job was easy:
plucking one leaf
from the calendar

The Kruegers Talk About the Dusty 30's

What she remembers most
is having to put the plates
upside down on the table
When you picked one up
it left a clean circle
on the oilcloth
                    That
and the time the black winds
blew her chicks over to Manitoba
"I cried all day," she says
but her husband wonders why —
"They must've felt at home
when we already sent across
forty acres for them to land on"

Lessons

Learn from your students I was told
and what have I learned from them

A woman's gasping rage against Wordsworth
taught me about cabin fever at thirty below
on a farm near Sylvan Lake, Alberta —
"the external World is fitted to the Mind" —
but she recalled the yard light burning blue
on snow that drifted up to the window sills
and that landscape would never fit her mind

From my deaf student I learned the feel
of my own voice
                            Her quick eyes on me
When I went blank turning to the board
or mumbled through lips held too close
("Open your mouth three fingers wide to sing"
but no one ever told me how many for speaking)
I began to sense the ambiguity
of voiced and unvoiced consonants
that invisible buzz in the larynx
Once in the hallway she plucked
my sleeve gently to get my attention
then asked a question in the stage whisper
of one unsure of her own volume

I still like Wordsworth's countryside
and the stoic dignity of his people
but I know the motions of my own speaking
through a persistent tug at my sleeve

Helpmeet

"The Sixties were not an age of innocence."

Wallace Stegner

I saw an old couple
moving cautiously on the icy pavement
of a parking lot, arm in arm,
and that image balanced against
my memory of the folk singer
who met visitors in bed
like a king of France, beside
his strung-out wife.
He would talk all morning
and when she tugged his arm
or whimpered like a sick puppy,
he would take a pill from the bottle
by the bed and place it under her tongue
without pausing in his night club patter.
Their dealer, he said, never sold anything
without trying it first.
But what balances the image
of Carol, spoonfeeding her needle-sick husband,
yellow eyes against a pillow, too weak
to move, the man who would kill her over money
a few months later, when he was strong enough.
I would need to know interlaced lives
as well as arms, how many years
of trust and comfort
to cancel the irony
of that patient spoon, dipping and lifting,
dipping and lifting.

Meeting and Parting

I saw my old teacher again
He'd lost faith in the academy
then turned to making books
He never lost faith in printing
sheaves of paper gathered and bound

He let me off at the hotel
and headed back for the country
where the dogs would be hungry
A victim of two strokes
but sure of his midnight way

I leaned on the balcony rail
thinking of the narrow highway
and watching the heated pool
In the cold mountain air
it carried a blanket of mist

We dwell at such a boundary

Harmonics

It's the shattered instrument
that gets the applause nowadays,

but try to swallow the universe
by turning yourself inside out

so that the farthest reaches
become your deepest spaces,

or consider the Irish harp: without
glue or fasteners, held together

not broken by its pressures.

Small Elegy

"Come quick," the older sister yells,

"Phyllis is sitting on a garbage bag
in the alley, singing to a dead bird."

What kind of idyll is this,
far from pastoral Greece?

We dispose of the dead sparrow
and lecture the child on decay.

"Will you explain to the cat?"
she asks — the gray killer last seen

honing its claws on a stump.

Milking Time

I begin to learn the organization of means
that sustains human appetite: the vacuum pump
draws milk from the udders of a dozen cows
into hoses leading up to clear pipe that runs
along the barn ceiling toward the cooling tank.
I watch the white liquid pulsing through tubes
and think of the vascular system of a huge animal.
But this network is superior, its arteries never
clog: when the milking operation is completed,
it cleanses itself with a flow of hot water.
No, compare the cow to an inefficient machine,
messy, irrational, a spotted blanket stretched
over a frame of ungainly bones. One producer
is out of phase, a breakdown: it's infected
and must be milked by the archaic squeeze-and-pull
into a battered bucket. The milk is waste, reserved
for the newly-weaned calves.
                                I go with the farmer
to their pen, where they crowd around the trough
like piglets at the side of a sow. Afterward,
instinct makes them bunch together, sucking fiercely
at each other's ears. The farmer singles out
a brown-faced bull calf and tells me, "That one's
for my freezer." The organization of means again,
a shelf is reserved for the stack of labeled packages
this being will become. And the brown-faced calf
keeps on sucking, one bright eye watching us.

The Snowball Koan

yesterday on a walk, watching
a clever man play fetch-it with a pup
snowballs tossed into a white drift

scurry of paws and tail, worried bark
was it a trick for the man to play
or for the dog to learn?

for Leslie Kawamura

Dandelion

Call me a weed, but flower, leaf and root will sustain you:
tear me out and I'll come again, begging a little room.
Fragility is my strength: a single breath
spreads me on the winds of the world.

The Familiar Animal

1

Note the horny tongue for combing the fur,
the broad whiskers that measure dark openings,
the fine hairs lining the rim of the ear flap
that make it twitch at the lightest intrusion.

No use for the pocket at the base of the ear,
unless you whimsically accept the fond opinion
that imagines a diminutive purse where the cat
hoards all the secrets that you whisper to it.

2

No, the secrets are safe because the holder
lives in another world. Once in a while my cat
walks up to the television and touches a paw
to the glass, wondering, "What's this warm box
purring in the corner." Then she walks away.

And in one of the slides I watched last night,
my daughter smiled in composure for the camera,
but the eyes of the cat she held like a baby
blazed demonic silver when the flash hit, meaning

"I am not in this picture,
I belong in another frame."

Cosmic Choreography

I move down my sister's driveway at midnight.
The tip of the car toes the line of the highway,
when on impulse I cut the lights. Before me,
the aurora borealis, green scrolls spread
in the northeastern sky, opening and closing,
fading and brightening, and all the while
I can hear music from my sister's stereo,
spiny constructions on the harpsichord. Somehow
the heavens are declaring the glory of Bach,
one intuition predicated. I'm feeling sleepy,
so my lights dim the spectacle, the motor
quells the music. I drive west, knowing
that back in town I'll make every green light
with the surest of touches on the pedals.

Queen of Saanich

White leviathan with a bellyful of buses,
cars and trucks, it moves into the strait,
course fixed and scheduled to the minute
I climb the stairs with the other passengers,
but most of them turn off toward the restaurant
where they'll spoon chowder and glance at the sea.
I walk on the sundeck alone, and find myself
drunk again on the air and last night's brandy.

The spinning radar dish by the smoke funnel
relentlessly guides us to a distant dock,
but the wind hits my hair in gusts, the gulls
come and go as they please, and all at once
a school of killer whales breaks the surface,
twenty at least, leaping in what must be joy —
these air breathers committed to the oceans,
their courses set for anywhere, arrival open.

for Jeanne Watchuk

Levels of Proficiency

A roomful of four year olds
painting on newsprint
spread on newspapers

One makes careful letters
learned from television
looped e's and dotted i's

Another makes a circle
bristling with spokes
all dashed off in blue

and says, "It's a sun,
a blue sun, and it's
a blue octopus too"

photo by William Tilland

Bert Almon lives in Edmonton and is a member of the English
Department of the University of Alberta. His first book of poems
THE RETURN was published by San Marcos Press in New Mexico
in 1968. Other books of poems he has published since then include
TAKING POSSESSION (1976) and POEMS FOR THE
NUCLEAR FAMILY (1979). Almon has lived in Alberta since
1968.

THISTLEDOWN BOOKS

WIND SONGS by Glen Sorestad

DARK HONEY by Ronald Marken

INSIDE IS THE SKY by Lorna Uher

OCTOMI by Andrew Suknaski

SUMMER'S BRIGHT BLOOD by William Latta

PRAIRIE PUB POEMS by Glen Sorestad

PORTRAITS by Lala Koehn

HAIL STORM by Peter Christensen

BETWEEN THE LINES by Stephen Scriver

GATHERING FIRE by Helen Hawley

TOWARDS A NEW COMPASS by Lorne Daniel

NOW IS A FAR COUNTRY by John V. Hicks

OLD WIVES LAKE by J. D. Fry

THE CURRIED CHICKEN APOCALYPSE by Michael Cullen

ANCESTRAL DANCES by Glen Sorestad

EAST OF MYLOONA by Andrew Suknaski

THE MUSHROOM JAR by Nancy Senior

BLUE SUNRISE by Bert Almon